MY SECRET MiLAN

A GIRL'S GUIDE TO INTIMATE MILAN

Marta Stella

MY SECRET MiLAN

A GIRL'S GUIDE TO INTIMATE MILAN

GREMESE

Original title: *My Secret Milan*
2013 © L'Airone

Cover: Costanza Agnese Matranga
Graphic design: Costanza Agnese Matranga,
in collaboration with Andrea Chiara De Santis
Photo credits: Nico K. Tucci

Translated from the Italian by: Miranda Lim

Printed and bound by: Conti Tipocolor – Calenzano (Fi)

2014 © Gremese
New Books s.r.l. – Roma
www.gremese.com

ISBN 978-88-7301-772-1

To my father.
To that day when we left the sea behind us,
to look upon this city from above.

THIS BOOK WOULD NEVER HAVE SEEN THE LIGHT IF...

Debora had not asked to meet at the coffee machine one morning in March.

Tea had not convinced me to go out for one more glass of vodka.

I had not met Kiyoe on a flight bound for Cyprus.

Costanza had not answered my phone call at 1 p.m. on April 6th.

I had not met the eccentric photographer Nico, who was wearing a feather headdress on that summer's day.

I had not persuaded a grumpy old bartender to fix me a daily cup of cappuccino to take away.

Benedetta had not pulled up her bike to tell me all about Studio 54 and stories of Milan in the old days, on a hot summer's day along the Naviglio Grande canal.

I had not talked about *The Sheltering Sky* with John Malkovich, whom I met by chance during Design Week on a couch in the Pecci Museum.

I had not run, hoped, struggled and had so many incredible encounters in this city's streets, and realized that with a dream and the right determination, anything is possible.

FOREWORD

Mapping out a city does not just mean retracing your steps, following the routes you know by heart and returning to familiar places: the rhythm of these day-to-day activities beats time with our routine like the hands of an urban clock. Instead, you have to infiltrate the city and gain insider access: that way, you can get to know its moods, customs, types and clichés, and try to find (great) beauty in the city, by looking at it afresh with new eyes.

Try to do the following: stop complaining constantly about the dull weather and the traffic, raise your eyes from your smartphone screen for a moment, and change your usual route by deliberately getting off at the wrong stop. Collect the stories of born-and-bred Milanese citizens, but also those people who came here by chance with a childhood dream or a challenge, those who have become new people here or who just came to have a little look round the city; those who have succeeded in finding a home here and those who are still searching; those who thought they had chosen the right path, but then decided to make an about-turn by changing course and reinventing themselves; those who had a random encounter – that spark that triggered a revolution – and who took over old sites to write their own personal story there.

The eight people I interviewed told me about their secret, intimate Milan through their memories and anecdotes. They cited the places that have inspired them and those which continue to do so: unmissable destinations and their own personal oases of peace. This little guide takes off from here: it is a compilation of some of Milan's most curious locations and maps a beautiful city that is full of contradictions. Although the inhabitants always complain about life in Milan, they know that they will never leave. If Milan was a woman, she would be the one sitting on her own at the end of a crowded table with her legs crossed. She would be rather aloof, severe, proud, self-assured, and sometimes a bit standoffish, yet ready to prove herself at any opportunity.

Ready for the tour? Little tip: if you don't want to follow the official route, you have to abandon yourself to fate. Simply open the book and follow your instinct: you might find a surprise waiting for you right at your fingertips. The colored dots next to the addresses refer to their category in the index, and you can use this book to carve out your own personalized and intimate map of the city.

CONTENTS
List of things to do in Milan:
Fashion and beauty

Small indulgences

Art, culture and design

Bars, cafes and restaurants

Ideas

Contributors

Learn the art of waiting

"Excuse me, I'm looking for 14 via Santa Marta. I think I'm lost…"
"You're in the right place. This is the Cinque Strade district. It's easy to get lost. But all you need to do is walk around in circles!"

Some people change their route on a daily basis and often find the perfect turning even at the most unexpected crossroads. Others prefer to concentrate on the present and simply wait for the right moment. This is a bit like taking that hidden side street, where the traffic disappears and the noises of the city fade away, albeit temporarily. You wait and wait for something that is sometimes just around the corner, ready to seize the moment.

So much for fans of the *carpe diem* way of life: here is a woman who has turned the philosophy upside-down. Uberta Zambeletti is a designer and fashion consultant for the biggest fashion houses. She took all those hours spent waiting during her travels and transferred them to an eighteenth-century former convent right in the heart of Milan.

According to Uberta, there are still some ghosts hanging around; they move secretly between unique pieces by young designers and vintage clothes from Paris or Tel Aviv. But if you have the patience to rummage through the small boxes scattered around the shop, you can find some real bargains. Sometimes, when everything leads you in a new direction, the real challenge is to stop, expect the unexpected and simply enjoy the wait. So wait and see!

Wait and See ●
via Santa Marta, 14 – 20123 Milan
Tel. 02 72080195
www.waitandsee.it waitandsee@waitandsee.it

Look at what's behind *that* door on the Navigli

Sometimes you might find the door to this place ajar, just waiting to be opened. Once you enter, you will find yourself in a small and verdant oasis. This haven of art and culture is a veritable gem hidden away in the bustling heart of the Navigli.

You will pass through a historic part of Milan to reach Spazio Cortina art gallery, by way of the Vicolo dei Lavandai, old artisan shops and a watchful painter who likes to observe casual passers-by through the open door of his studio. If you want to put a busy day on silent mode and forget about all those emails from your boss that await you on your smartphone, this is the perfect place. No doorbell, no invitation required. No one will ask you who you are or why you are there. What a marvel! Entrance is free for all: art lovers, experts and incognito observers alike. This is the perfect chance to pose as that famous art curator looking for new pieces for her private collection. A place never lacking in ambiance, against a cool jazz background.

Spazio Cortina ●
vicolo dei Lavandai, 2 – 20144 Milan
Naviglio Grande
www.spaziocortina.com
info@spaziocortina.com

Get a makeover in a living room-cum-hair salon

We all like to exchange snippets of our life online, labeling our thoughts with hashtags. Whatsapp enables us to transform emoticons into a virtual and silent surrogate for real conversation. But let's admit it: who doesn't dream every now and then of going back to the days of those old fancy get-togethers? So here's my advice for all you girls who are feeling nostalgic for the exclusive locations of a bygone era, those parlors where chic ladies and fashionable bon vivants exchanged closely guarded secrets in hidden corners of the city. If this is what you're after, Davide Diodovich's *The Studio* is the place to go.

After working for hairstyling guru Vidal Sassoon, Davide decided to turn his Milan apartment into the city's most exclusive hair salon. The apartment is located on the ground floor of a historic building. Once you've made your reservation, you will find yourself surrounded by Fornasetti's faces and autographed pictures of Mina, the Italian singer. Color expert Susanna Celin will totally transform your look. Insider tip: if you come here during Milan Fashion Week, you could find yourself chatting with Garance Doré over a cup of tea – behind closed doors, of course!

The Studio by Davide Diodovich ●
via Torquato Tasso, 4 – 20123 Milan
Tel. 02 89283420
www.davidediodovich.it
thestudio@davidediodovich.com

TRAVEL BACK IN TIME

Imagine the past life of a seventies skirt. Use the shop windows as your mirror, and admire yourself in a retro cap that once belonged to one very chic Milanese lady. Dream about items that are twice your age and rummage in the pockets of a camel coat. Even if you leave home without a plan, you can still return with a piece of fifties jewelry, which is sure to become your favorite new talisman. Here's how to travel back in time – in your wardrobe.

Shop for charity
Humana Vintage ●
via Cappellari, 3 – 20123 Milan
Tel. 02 72080606
www.humanavintage.it
smistamento@humanavintage.it

Meet the vintage collector
Franco Jacassi
Vintage Delirium ●
via Giuseppe Sacchi, 3 – 20121 Milan
Tel. 02 86462076
www.vintagedeliriumfj.com
info@vintagedeliriumfj.com

Join a traveling circus
for a day
Circolo delle Pulci ●
The location is only revealed shortly
before by email.
www.ilcircodellepulci.com

Buy an old print
Antiques Market ●
Every last Sunday of the month
except July.
www.naviglilive.it

Rediscover the art of buying and selling
Bivio Milano ●
via Gian Giacomo Mora, 4 – 20123 Milan
Tel. 02 58108691
www.biviomilano.it
info@biviomilano.it

Lose yourself in a vinyl collection
Serendeepity ●
corso di Porta Ticinese, 100 – 20123 Milan
Tel. 02 89400420
www.serendeepity.net
info@serendeepity.net

Put yourself in a retro mood
Lipstick Vintage ●
corso Garibaldi, 79 – 20119 Milan
Tel. 02 63086165

Find a vintage Chanel bag
Memory Lane ●
via Galeazzo Alessi, 8 – 20123 Milan
Tel. 02 39542764

Track down an Eisenberg bracelet
Madame Pauline Vintage ●
Foro Buonaparte, 74 – 20121 Milan
Tel. 02 49431201
www.madamepaulinevintage.it
madamepaulinevintage@gmail.com

Look at the world through the lenses of 70's glasses
Foto Veneta Ottica ●
via Torino, 57 – 20123 Milan
Tel. 02 8055735

Stop by a vintage collector's paradise
Cavalli e Nastri ●
via Brera, 2 – 20121 Milan
Tel. 02 72000449
via Gian Giacomo Mora,
3-12 – 20123 Milan
Tel. 02 89409452
www.cavallienastri.com

Visit a 40's barber's shop
20134 Lambrate ●
via Conte Rosso,
22 – 20134 Lambrate
Tel. 02 91533992
www.20134lambrate.it
20134lambrate@gmail.com

23

"*My Milan is a very hectic one; the one I've got to know by running from one end of the city to the other for my work. But in those rare moments free from meetings or other commitments, I love to stop by Cavalli e Nastri, an amazing vintage shop, or to have lunch at Sushi Zero, a divine Japanese restaurant. After an exhausting day, I always dream of spending the evening on the terrace of Giacomo Arengario's restaurant, which overlooks the Museo del Novecento, and which offers a perfect view of the Duomo all lit up at night.*"

Livia Firth, creative director of Eco Age

Whisper in an artist's ear

How many times have you wanted to say something in the ear of your favorite artist and share a secret with them that you have confided to no one else, or to ask them an awkward question that no one has ever dared ask? Unfortunately, like many conversations with idols, the answer may disappoint you. But it's definitely worth a try!

Fancy giving it go? Head to 10 via Serbelloni: this is the entrance to a building from the 1920s that has earned the nickname of "Ca' de l'oreggia", as they say in Milan, or "The ear house". To the right of the door there is a large bronze ear, forged by the hands of artist Adolfo Wildt. Are you ready to whisper a secret that you have never told anyone else?

Orecchio di Wildt ●
via Gabrio Serbelloni, 10 – 20122 Milan

Attend a play in a gallery

So, now you know: in Milan, finding something new and exciting just right around the corner is the first rule of survival. You have to look beyond appearances and discover all those hidden details that you have never noticed before. It's time to start looking for that unexpected corner; only then will you begin to discover a whole new city. Follow your own personal itineraries; they will become part of your secret road map for each day.

Walk along Corso Buenos Aires, and then stop at number 33. Here, a little gallery will lead you to a famous venue for theatre and culture. This is the home of a Milanese theater company that has won renown ever since its foundation in the seventies, and whose current home is a room from the thirties. The theatre was originally established under the name of Teatro dell'Elfo, but was renamed Teatro Elfo Puccini in 2010. The Shakespeare Room is the perfect place to catch a contemporary play, or else you can head to the Fassbinder room for a more intimate performance, or to the Bausch room for a dance show. If you arrive early, you can pass the time with a quick coffee or dine surrounded by the poems on the walls in the bar of the foyer.

Teatro Elfo Puccini
corso Buenos Aires, 33 – 20124 Milan
Tel. 02 00660606
www.elfo.org

ENJOY A NIGHT AT THE THEATRE

With the three pillars of Milan's theatre history
Piccolo Teatro Strehler
Largo Antonio Greppi, 1 – 20121 Milan
Tel. 848 800304

Piccolo Teatro Grassi
via Rovello, 2 – 20121 Milan
Tel. 848 800304

Piccolo Teatro Studio
via Rivoli, 6 – 20121 Milan
Tel. 848 800304
www.piccoloteatro.org

With a traditional choice
Teatro Litta
corso Magenta, 24 – 20123 Milan
Tel. 02 8055882
www.teatrolitta.it

With a historic institution
Teatro Manzoni
via Alessandro Manzoni,
42 – 20121 Milan
Tel. 02 7636901
www.teatromanzoni.it

With a tribute
Teatro Franco Parenti
via Giorgio Vasari, 15 – 20135 Milan
Tel. 02 599951
www.teatrofrancoparenti.it

With a classical music concert
Teatro dal Verme
via San Giovanni sul Muro,
2 – 20121 Milan
Tel. 02 87905
www.dalverme.org

With a lyric opera
Nuovo Teatro degli Arcimboldi
viale dell'Innovazione,
20 – 20126 Milan
Tel. 02 641142212/02 641142214
www.teatroarcimboldi.it

With a traditional tale from the 19th century
Teatro Carcano
corso di Porta Romana,
63 – 20122 Milan
Tel. 02 55181377
www.teatrocarcano.com

With new languages in a former church of the Inquisition
Teatro Arsenale
via Cesare Correnti, 11 – 20123 Milan
Tel. 02 832199
www.teatroarsenale.it

VOGLIO
PIÙ SPA-
ZIO PER
L'ARTE

Dine in the city's smallest bistro

What can you do with 19 square meters? If it's a room in a shared apartment, you can move in your entire world and pretend to star in the remake of *The Spanish Apartment*. In a studio flat, you can create a *room of your very own* that would make even Saint Virginia Woolf proud.

Alessandro Lo Piccolo and Giancarlo Petriglia have taken a different approach by turning this tiny space into the city's smallest bistro, which you can find by turning off piazza Argentina and stopping at the corner of via Niccolò Paganini. Here you won't fail to notice the long red carpet, the retro tables, colorful rabbits and large letters on the ground; *benvenute a The Small*, welcome to The Small. Furnished halfway between a bazaar and an antiques shop, you can dine alongside the other diners seated at small neighbouring tables. You will be immersed in an atmosphere that combines thirties teapots, unique pieces and a speckled version of Anna Wintour's face.

Everything is for sale, except the crockery and cutlery. Next door is the Plus_P + Petriglia, or "the new room", as the hosts like to call it: an intimate lounge where good food combines with the pleasure of being surrounded by artwork and bags by Giancarlo. Designers, journalists, fashion editors and PR all gather here after work: *the* place to go for all the week's gossip.

The Small ●
via Niccolò Paganini, 3 – 20124 Milan
Open Tuesday to Sunday.
Tel. 02 20240943
www.thesmall.it
info@thesmall.it

29

Watch a movie at a nail bar with friends

"I wanted to create a place where every woman could have that little extra something, so that she could do several things at once in the limited free time left to her in her busy day."

These days we like to display our dreams and passions to the world with a like on Facebook. We share them every day from our smartphones or classify them on our Pinterest boards. But Gaia has managed to enclose them all in a single beauty box: a small nail salon around the corner from piazza XXIV Maggio. This is a beauty and clothing oasis where every Milanese woman can indulge in a well-earned break.

Gaia created Bahama Mama partly for fun and partly for the challenge of fulfilling her dream. Today it is a Mecca for journalists, bloggers, busy women and groups of girlfriends who get together for a weekly drink after work. Relax with a manicure session whilst sipping an organic cocktail or watching a movie. Leaf through *Marie Claire* at your leisure and browse the unique vintage pieces carefully selected by Gaia. The waiting list is always off limits and you must ring the doorbell to enter. Also, don't forget to book.

Bahama Mama ⬤
viale Col di Lana, 1 – 20136 Milan
Tel. 02 89404538
www.bahamamama.it
info@bahamamama.it

Treat yourself to a cupcake

Let's face it. Who hasn't dreamed of being able to change their life overnight? Who hasn't thought of changing jobs, routines or habits? To just throw ourselves into a new project: our own. To experiment with new worlds and leave our comfort zone for the unknown. This is what comes to mind after a bad day. It's only natural. But even when things have gone well and we feel ready to conquer the world in Wonder Woman's corset and with a force that not even Bionic Woman can match.

This is the story of Lucia, a former economist, who has since become Milan's Queen of Cupcakes. After gaining a degree in Economics and beginning a career in fashion communication, she decided to drop everything and devote herself to her dream of opening a small bakery in the heart of the district of Brera. She is assisted by Pina, her chef mom, who has supported her and who has been part of the project from the start. The idea was to set up a little corner of sweetness in the city that would offer a range of sugared and iced confections and homemade desserts. If you want to feel inspired by someone who has courageously followed their goal, this is the place. Breathe in the delicious aromas wafting from the kitchen as you sink your spoon into a slice of freshly baked cake and treat yourself to a cup of tea.

Di Viole di Liquirizia ●
via Madonnina, 10 – 20121 Milan
Tel. 02 89092201
Closed on Mondays.
www.diviolediliquirizia.it

Near Manee
Brera

Have a slice of cake in a garden center

If you are not blessed with a green thumb, the place to start taking your first lessons is located just a stone's throw away from the San Lorenzo Columns. If you turn into via Gian Giacomo Mora, you will find a special hidden atelier: a garden center dedicated to garden designs with a high sugar content.

Here you will be welcomed by a small woman with a fiery red bob and vivacious manner: get ready to meet the true Queen of Plants, Antonella. She is assisted by her daughter Fara, who is also a garden designer. Together they have created a luxury nursery where you can choose new plants for your room or balcony. Those with the means can even find solutions for gardens in the city. In the meantime, you can sample a slice of pear cake or a dried fruit donut, prepared in Saint Bioeus patisserie in Monza by the owner's son.

Gardenia ●
via Gian Giacomo Mora, 20 – 20123 Milan
Tel. 02 58115241
www.gardeniasas.it
info@gardeniasas.it

Sleep in an art gallery

You've just got back from a vernissage. A little pit stop after work, where you alternate between getting drinks, greeting friends and asking who the artist is. Yet this is a miracle cure for clearing your mind after a busy day. You met a friend of a friend, *that* artist, the up-and-coming writer who you "absolutely must read", and that indie musician – if you don't listen to his music you are so "out". But the only thing that sticks in your mind is that corner towards the end of the exhibition: you dream of buying that painting for your room or living room.

There is a simple solution: spend the night at 18 Via Sacchini, a unique B&B and 24 hour art gallery, where you can sleep surrounded by the artwork on sale. This project was born from the idea of two people with a shared love for hospitality and two stories that became one. Alberto and Raul took over a former car repair shop in the Loreto area to create their haven, which is open to visitors, friends and travelers passing through the city. This is a collection of unusual objects, mementos from their childhood homes and exotic travels. Once you have taken the signal red lift, the hosts, like gallerists presenting their new exhibition, will guide you to one of the three guest rooms, each with a different story to tell. Then you can head up to the large terrace on the top floor and enjoy the sunset over Milan. You will feel right at home.

RossoSegnale and 3001 Lab ●
via Antonio Sacchini, 18 – 20131 Milan
Tel. 02 29527453
www.rossosegnale.it
info@rossosegnale.it
3001lab@rossosegnale.it

Have brunch with a circus queen in a former shoemaker's workshop

Can you picture those large posters announcing the arrival of Italy's most famous circus? They're brightly colored, usually vivid fuchsia, and are taken up by the giant face of the Italian circus queen, Moira Orfei. This is the artwork that artist Sunny Asemota created as a gift for his landlord Angelo. Angelo then decided to exhibit the art in the main room of his bistro.

An interior designer with a passion for cooking, Angelo took over a former shoemaker's workshop and transformed it into what is now an obligatory food stop if you ever find yourself in the Via Tortona area. It is a favorite meeting point for the fashion showroom crowd, and a symbolic crossroads for the Fuori Salone events that take place during Milan Design Week.

The perfect venue to go with friends for brunch or a dinner of traditional Italian dishes. Also, if you want to see that (unmissable) film that has been snubbed by mainstream cinema, you will find an excellent place for avant-garde cinema right next door. After dinner at Angelo's, a trip to Cinema Mexico is a must.

Angelo's Bistrot ⬤
via Savona, 55 – 20144 Milan
Tel. 02 45548642

Dine with Peter Lindbergh

"Seriously, you don't know Torre di Pisa? It's my favorite restaurant! You should definitely try it. It's fantastic!"

Peter Lindbergh addressed these words to a group of journalists and onlookers on a sunny afternoon in early September. They were arranged in a semicircle around him, having rushed to meet the great photographer in the courtyard of number 10 corso Como, a few hours before his exhibition launch. Mr. Lindbergh discussed the women he had photographed, Jeanne Moreau, the perfect shot and Paris, his hometown. Once the conversation shifted to his favorite places to eat, his immediate response was Brera.

If you fancy meeting him on one of his stopovers in Milan, you'll have to go to a historic inn on Via Fiori Chiari. In the seventies, many of Milan's bohemians graced its tables, and the inn has also played host to Accademia di Brera events for many years. They say that Ettore Sottsass used to dine here, and even Andy Warhol would come when he was in town.

Today, just as in the old days, you'll find Milan's jet set and creative talents here, such as "Purple" Magazine's founder, who loves to come here to capture its diners with classic black and white shots, which he then posts on his blog.

Torre di Pisa ●
via Fiori Chiari, 21 – 20121 Milan
Tel. 02 874877
www.trattoriatorredipisa.it

Treat yourself to a bouquet of takeaway flowers

Today men have somewhat lost their way. It's a fact. They are ever more disorientated in the face of female empowerment, yet they still don't want to give up the search for their perfect other half. That is, the eternal chimera of the Alfa male, who is harder to find than the Holy Grail. But how do you get around this without unnecessary preamble or having to resort to theoretical manuals? For those of you who still dream that a romantic gift will be waiting secretly for you on your office desk or by your front door, here you can practice the saying: "If you want a thing done well, do it yourself".

The practice session takes place at 18 Corso Giuseppe Garibaldi, in a space measuring twenty square meters, which spills out onto the sidewalk, coloring it green. This is a small florist that goes by the name of Frida's, and here you can discover how treating yourself can really make your day. This place supplies flowers for stylists on photo shoots, fashion editors and party planners. But casual passers-by can also pop in and return home with a bouquet wrapped in paper like a baguette: a gift from you to you.

Frida's ⬤
corso Giuseppe Garibaldi, 18 – 20121 Milan
Tel. 02 8900307
www.fridas.it

INVEST YOUR SAVINGS IN ...

Precious jewels
Pellini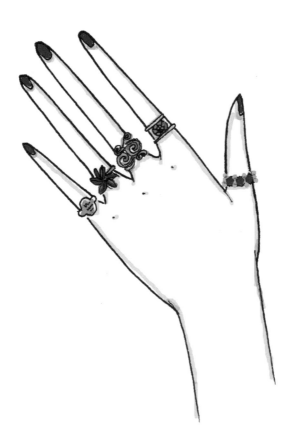
via Alessandro Manzoni,
20 – 20121 Milan
Tel. 02 76008084
www.pellini.it
manzoni@pellini.it

A lucky charm
Anaconda
via Bergamini,
7 – 20122 Milan
Tel. 02 58325684
www.anacondamilano.com
info@anacondamilano.com

Handmade jewelry
Atelier VM
via Cesare Correnti,
26 – 20136 Milan
Tel. 02 43118105
www.ateliervm.com
info@ateliervm.com

*A creation by a young
female Italian jewelry
designer*
Segni di Gi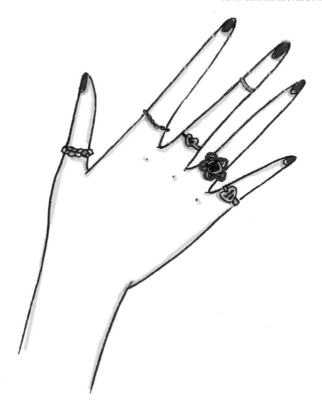
*via Ausonio, 6
– 20123 Milan
Tel. 340 3513206
www.segnidigi.com
gi@segnidigi.com*

A pair of unique cufflinks
Demaldè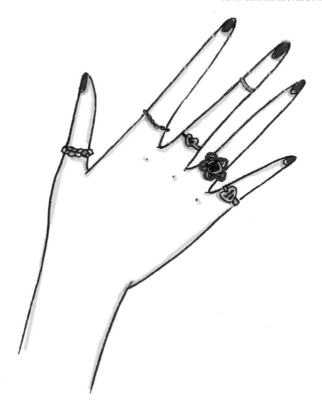
*via Ponte Vetero, 22
– 20121 Milan
Tel. 02 86460428*

*A vintage ring from a
Flea Market*
**Porta Genova Flea
Market**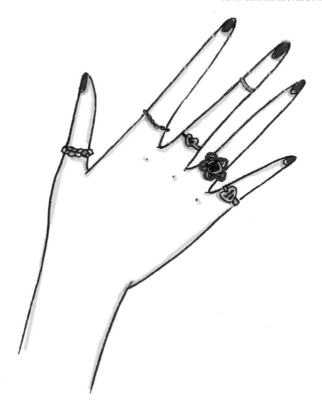
*Every Sunday
via Valenza, 6
– 20144 Milan
Tel. 02 43118105
www.facebook.com/
IlMercatinoDiPortaGenova*

The perfect flats
Porselli ●
piazza Paolo Ferrari,
6 – 20121 Milan
Tel. 02 8053759
www.porselli.it
info@porselli.it

Mens' silver loafers
Stiù ●
corso di Porta Ticinese,
105 – 20123 Milan
Tel. 02 8322018
www.stiu.it

A pair of Acne Studio boots
Frip ●
corso di Porta Ticinese,
16 – 20123 Milan
Tel. 02 8321360
www.frip.it
info@frip.it

A young and (little) known brand
Tug Store ●
via Muratori, 28 – 20135 Milan
Tel. 02 36550244
www.tugstore.it
info@tugstore.it

Bon-ton sandals
Suede ●
via Cesare Correnti,
21 – 20123 Milan
Tel. 02 36597591
www.suede.it
info@suede.it

A cocktail dress
Imarika ●
via Giovanni Morelli,
1 – 20129 Milan
Tel. 02 76005268
www.imarika.com
info@imarika.com

A new up-and-coming designer
Wok Store ●
viale Col di Lana,
5 – 20136 Milan
Tel. 02 89829700
www.wok-store.com
info@wok-store.com

Tour the world with this year's most beautiful photos

You may have come across some of these shots while reading an article in the pages of a monthly magazine one Sunday morning over a leisurely cup of coffee. You tweeted the ones that caught your eye. Or maybe you flicked through some of the photos in an online gallery that features that month's most beautiful photos. Those images that capture breathtaking moments, freeze-frames that become part of history and facts that shock the world.

Every year, after the official award ceremony and a tour of the world's biggest cities, the shots from the *World Press Photo* are displayed in the Carla Sozzani gallery in Milan at 10 corso Como. This unique spot incorporates art, avant-garde, fashion and relaxation in the environs of a green haven. Once you step inside this bookshop, you will never want to leave.

World Press Photo at the Carla Sozzani Gallery ●
corso Como, 10 – 20154 Milan
Tel. 02 653531
www.galleriacarlasozzani.org

"*I'm Milanese through and through. Maurizio Cattelan, who's always travelling, introduced me to a traditional trattoria in the ethnic heart of Porta Venezia. He had his birthday party there a few years ago. It's called il Carpaccio and it's on via Lazzaro Palazzi, right next to what was once one of Milan's most exciting artistic hubs back in the nineties. Today, a 40 cm deep window is nestled between the restaurant and this former artistic space, and artists can experiment freely here, without restrictions of any kind. What's more, space is not an issue, as they can spill out onto the road if they wish.*
Each opening turns into a full-scale public party; anyone can attend, whether they're a guest or simply passing by. There's room for everyone. As Myriam Ben Salah wrote on Artforum.com: 'Nothing to sell but lots to admire – food, art, sparkling wine and, of course, Prosecco. The sidewalks were cheerfully crowded and Milan never looked so alive to me'."

Caroline Corbetta,
curator and director of Crepaccio

Dance the tango with Cattelan

A live orchestra plays with gusto, and the players' smiles never waver. The dancers' quick steps keep time to an old classic. You can hear the music long before you even cross the threshold. A symbolic voyage into a far-off world: now seems the moment to start the time machine. The atmosphere is nostalgic: it recalls post-war Italy, where people gathered in dance halls to celebrate the rebirth of music and gin. Today this place is a fusion of different eras and the revival of milonga and boogie sets the trend of understatement. If you want to find a fashionable spot, Sala Venezia is the place to go.

Once you've signed up, you can surrender to an evening under the twinkling little lights drawn over the dance floor like rainbows, and step to the glowing beat of silver strobes. Try a homemade *crostata* at the gingham covered tables. There will be a flurry of feet next to you: pairs of lifelong dance partners, one-time porters and young dancers simply there by chance. You could even find yourself dancing the tango with Cattelan, the famous artist, who used this dance hall for "Toilet Paper" magazine's party.

When the weather's nice, the Sala's guests move outside to the Balera dell'Ortica, a corner of Milan that appears to be suspended in time, where you can have *arrosticini* under an illuminated pergola, before moving onto the dance floor. Dance under the lights of a midsummer night, accompanied by old-timers and new tableaux vivants from the city.

Sala Venezia ●
via Alvise Cadamostro,
2 – 20129 Milan
Tel. 02 70128680

Balera dell'Ortica ●
via Giovanni Antonio Amadeo,
78 – 20133 Milan
Tel. 02 70128680

DISCOVER THE CITY'S GREEN SPOTS WITH...

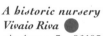

A historic nursery
Vivaio Riva ●
via Arena, 7 – 20123 Milan
Tel. 02 58101141

A vegetarian takeaway
Lattughino ●
via Lodovico il Moro, 3 – 20143 Milan
Tel. 02 87280181
www.lattughino.it
info@lattughino.it

A zero-impact restaurant
LifeGate Café ●
via della Commenda, 43 – 20122 Milan
Tel. 02 5450765
www.lifegate.it

A flower show
Orticola – Flower market and show
Indro Montanelli Public Gardens ●
via Palestro – 20121 Milan
www.orticola.org

"I will always be indebted to Mauro Bellini, one of the owners of this lovely hair salon, Les Garçons de la Rue. He practically saved my life by showing me where to get plastic hairpins, which I had never been able to find in the right size before. Previously, the metal hairpins I always wore set off the metal detectors at every airport I traveled through (and there are many pins and many airports). It always caused me a nightmare by beeping and resulted in guards doing an undignified rummage through my hair. Now, I have plastic hairpins and no more hassle.

Moving on to via Manzoni, I like to stop by Radaelli (at no. 16), because I love flowers and I especially love their selection, the quality of service and the attention to detail. That 'je ne sais quoi' factor of this florist makes it a destination in itself. The Triennale Design Museum is another one of my favorites: aside from being a wonderful museum, I was really happy that I was able to screen the fifth edition of my ASVOFF festival there. It was a brief home away from home and a creative engine that inspired me and my guests."

Diane Pernet, founder and director of A Shaded View on Fashion Film

Have a coffee in a florist-bar

You love Milan, but you dream of whiling away your evenings on the steps of the Paris Opera, perhaps to watch the strangers who meet there to dance the tango together in the setting sun. Then you spend a weekend in Paris and you find yourself missing Milan: Brera's little streets, the light of piazza Duomo in the morning. And deep down, you even miss all those people who never stop complaining about life in Milan, yet who secretly adore their city.

7 via Montebello is where you want to go to soak up this sort of atmosphere. Originally home to a florist, it is now a romantic bar and restaurant, where bouquets adorn the tables and shelves against a quaint white backdrop. When you step into this haven, *Violà*! you're in France.

Fioraio Bianchi Caffè ●
via Montebello, 7 – 20121 Milan
Tel. 02 29014390
www. fioraiobianchicaffe.it
info@fioraiobianchicaffe.it

Wear a hat like a work of art

Every woman should give this a go at least once in her life, especially those women who wouldn't know a buttonhole from a trouser hem! Choose the perfect fabric for your ideal dress. Tell your favorite stylist about your dream creation; they will take your rough idea and use it to design an article that is made-to-measure. Come with a story to tell and watch as it is transformed into an accessory that you can keep forever.

The woman to go to in Milan for all this is Krisztina Reisini. Krisztina is a Hungarian creator with a cosmopolitan soul, having travelled all over the world, moving from London to Paris and from Los Angeles to New York, before settling in Milan. Today you'll find her showroom at 14 via Tortona: when you get there, ring for Kreisicouture.

Kreisicouture Atelier ●
via Tortona, 14 – 20144 Milan
Tel. 02 49517273
www.kreisicouture.com
info@kreisicouture.com

Travel to Russia

It's one of those evenings when the tram is running late and it's raining. You look awful and can't wait to get back to your pad. You then decide to change course by heading to that secluded spot that is home to a small core group of regulars. The result: after a few months, you realize that the trusty barman is a great listener: he's your new favorite confidant!

For those who love those wintry hideouts where you can have an intimate chat with a close friend, number 6 via Vittadini is the place to go, just around the corner from Ravizza park. As you enter, you will find yourself in a small cavern with red walls. On your right, a notice written in block capitals reads: PRAVDA, the truth. Coincidence?

Frog will be waiting to greet you behind the bar: just look for the man with the tattooed arms. He has created a veritable cocktail culture with his expert dexterity. He used to work as head barman at Yar, the historic Russian restaurant in Milan, before deciding to open up his own place with the help of his partner Andrea. And their bar is a real gem.

Little tip: get your host to tell you a story whilst you sip a vodka Gimlet.

Pravda Vodka Bar ●
via Carlo Vittadini, 6 – 20136 Milan

Go radical chic

That crowded, popular bar is not your scene: too many people – always the same faces. No, just no. And that retro place is just *too* vintage and trendy – it doesn't do it for you at all. If you don't fit into either of these categories, why not make your way to 30 via Paolo Sarpi?

The Isola Wine Cellars will welcome you with a selection of some of the city's best wines. It's better to go during the week, so you can avoid the weekend rush.

Cantine Isola ●
via Paolo Sarpi, 30 – 20154 Milan
Tel. 02 3315249

Experiment with the avant-garde in a former factory

There are few other places on the move where the coordinates of a story are continually reinvented like they are in the city, and where balance changes the destiny of events so rapidly. Sometimes we suddenly realize that our point of reference has taken down its bright sign overnight: our favorite bar is under new management. Here stories intertwine, whether for economic or historical reasons or out of necessity, amalgamating past experiences and far-off plans. Here's the good news: new spaces evolve, incorporating a mosaic of new objectives; it seems like a revival was waiting just around the corner after that initial pause.

The story of Carminati, Toselli & Co. began in 1899, at number 4 via Giulio Procaccini. Milan city council used the factory to build trams for the public transport network, and the materials for the railways and tram tracks were all produced and repaired here too. But this all came to an end in 1935: the factory was sold and the new owners decided to pursue a new path. The turning point came in 1985, when Palazzo Marino decided to buy this glorious industrial site, and thus the Fabbrica del Vapore was born. Workshops, exhibitions, performances and receptions that are dedicated to modern art and aimed especially at young people, all take place under its high ceilings and outdoors under hammered iron canopies. If you're looking for the avant-garde, you're in the right place.

La Fabbrica del Vapore ●
via Giulio Procaccini, 4 – 20154 Milan
Tel. 02 88464130
www.fabbricadelvapore.org

61

Have a cup of good cheer

"Oh, hello doctor! Are you well?"
"And what are you doing here on a Sunday morning all by yourself, Miss? Are you going to marry one of these days, or not?!"

If there's a spot in Milan where traditional customs of a bygone era don't feel too outdated, the café on the corner of piazzale di Porta Lodovica is the place. Little tables with pink cotton tablecloths are arranged in a line on the pavement, each one set just so. Uniformed waiters move deftly between the tables and the bar, which is always packed. Someone might enter greeting everyone like neighbors; another might choose to sit at the bar in the evening, sipping an aperitif. When summer arrives, you might find a man in his shirtsleeves by the door, politely greeting customers as they go past, welcoming people entering and saying farewell to all those leaving the café.

Domenico Gattullo and his son have chosen to continue a proud family tradition that stretches back over fifty years, one which began in Ruvo di Puglia before coming to Milan. Jannacci, Gaber, Cochi and Renato, Beppe Viola and the Derby comedians have all been customers here. Today the bar is as bustling as ever, beginning with breakfast, which is not be missed. If you want to start the day with a smile, have a coffee and a *cannoncino alla crema*.

Gattullo ●
piazzale di Porta Lodovica, 2 – 20136 Milan
Tel. 02 58310497
www.gattullo.it
info@gattullo.it

Transform your evening in a flash

It's no myth that being in a rush is a way of life in Milan. Although in the dreamy evenings you may feel like Annie Hall in the metropolis, or a romantic wanderer returning home at sunset, you're actually always in a hurry. Sometimes it can be difficult to get out of the same old routine of home-work-home. You often spend your evenings curled up under your duvet on your trusty sofa, as though you were starring in the *Bridget Jones* remake or like Lena Dunham in *Girls*. Never fear: you can transform any quiet evening into the highlight of your week in no time at all. Just don't forget to put your favorite pair of shoes in your bag.

Why not drop everything and take a detour to piazza della Scala? Your change of plans will lead you straight to the ticket office. Once inside, there's nothing for it but to ask if there are any tickets left for the open rehearsals. This is a low-cost solution if you fancy hearing a concert preview, as this is the theatre orchestra's dress rehearsal before the real thing.
You could find yourself sitting with other audience members in a red velvet upper-tier box, next to a chic couple in their forties who are pretending to talk to one another or two fancy old ladies who are leaning over the balcony, discussing the names, surnames and dates of birth of all the passers-by. Worth a try.

Teatro alla Scala
via Filodrammatici, 2 – 20121 Milan
Tel. 02 72003744
www.teatroallascala.org

Take a coffee break with a flamingo

Sometimes all your friends are busy, and there's nowhere to sit in your favorite café. On days like this, why not spend some time with a flamingo?

Yes, that's right: a flamingo. This silent, pastel pink-colored companion (who is probably more of a Milanese citizen by now than you are), is perfect company. If you want to meet your flamingo, all you need to do is head to number 3 via Cappuccini and peek through the iron mesh that marks the borders of villa Invernizzi, a large private garden. For over thirty years, generations of flamingoes have roamed about here undisturbed, under the care of a trusty warden. Welcome to the first in a series of lessons on the balancing act of silence!

Villa Invernizzi ●
via Cappuccini, 3 – 20122 Milan

FIND A PAIR OF SHOES STRAIGHT OFF THE CATWALK

Those wooden platform shoes certainly didn't pass you by: they were look no. 27 at the last fashion show. That little coat that you've been chasing after for a year might be a bit more affordable now. That bag that is set to become a small capital investment is finally on sale. This stock is unmissable – you'll be able to grab yourself a real bargain.

Marni Outlet ●
via Filippo Tajani, 1 – 20133 Milan
Tel. 02 700009735
www.marni.com

Il Salvagente ●
via Fratelli Bronzetti, 16 – 20129 Milan
Tel. 02 76110328
www.salvagentemilano.it

10 Corso Como Outlet ●
via Enrico Tazzoli, 3 – 20154 Milan
Tel. 02 2901513
www.10corsocomo.com

D Magazine Outlet ●
via Bigli, 4 – 20121 Milan
Tel. 02 36643888
www.dmagazine.it

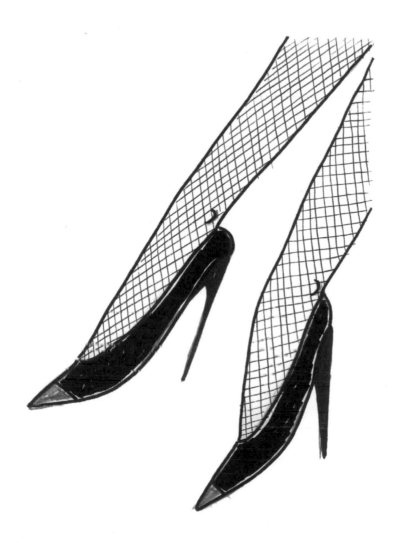

Enjoy a Martini as you 'fly' over the city

You've climbed to the top of historical monuments, churches and skyscrapers in the world's biggest cities. If you want to feel the same sense of exhilaration while in Milan, 7 piazza Diaz is your place. Once inside, step into the elevator and press the button for the fifteenth floor. The door will open, and if it's a sunny day you will be hit by a dazzling light radiating from the enormous windows: the type of light that is so loved by actresses during photocalls, as it makes them look even more beautiful.

This terrace is on the top floor of a skyscraper located a stone's throw from the Duomo. In the evening, the terrace transforms into one of the city's most exclusive spots: a red carpet is rolled out, and the air is filled with the flashes of photographers looking for that perfect shot. In the mornings, interviews are conducted in the lounge, where Italian directors mingle with journalists desperate to chat about this or that director's latest film.

The aerial paradise on the fifteenth floor is the ideal place to admire the Duomo's spires and the ant-like people below. As you sip your Martini, you can feel as if you've got the whole city in your hands.

Terrazza Martini ●
piazza Armando Diaz, 7 – 20122 Milan
www.martinierossi.it

Buy a Milan–Tokyo–São Paulo plane ticket

Get ready for a whirlwind adventure: you will leave Linate on a flight bound for Japan, stopping via Brazil for the second leg. When you get back to Milan, head to the left bank of the Naviglio Grande or 59 corso Garibaldi.

This has all the makings of a harebrained scheme of an equally harebrained travel agency. However, this will simply be your route once you enter Temakinho, Milan's first Brazilian sushi bar. Here you will experience a fusion of exotic flavors, which encompasses the migration history of a people and a cuisine that has greatly influenced a number of tastes and traditions. Tuck into the avocado *temaki* and vegetable sushi and take a sip of centrifuged juice, as you tap your foot under the table in time with the Bossa Nova playlist.

Temakinho – Brazilian sushi bar ●
Ripa di Porta Ticinese, 37 – 20143 Milan
Tel. 02 8356134
corso Giuseppe Garibaldi, 59 – 20121 Milan
Tel. 02 72016158
www.temakinho.com

Meet a young writer

He'll be instantly recognizable. He's sitting alone in a secluded corner, some distance away from the blue bar. Then he gets up and orders a glass of red wine. The usual. He sits down once more and does the following: he leafs through a newspaper, checks his mail on his smartphone, and tweets that day's news. He adjusts his glasses and sorts out his untidy locks. He checks his notifications and posts a comment, maybe a vitriolic one that says no, he completely disagrees.

This is the young writer of your dreams. Someone you might meet by chance in this small, welcoming bar, which is a local haunt for regulars in the Isola neighborhood. You might also find him here in the mornings, drinking a coffee chosen from the handwritten menu, eating a croissant and listening to the smooth jazz playing in the background.

Blu Bar ●
via Francesco Carmagnola, 5 – 20159 Milan
www.blumilano.net

frittelle di mele

FARINA

VanigliaInStecche

LATTE

e limoni

mele

zucchero

UOVA

BUONGIORNO!

(Good morning!)

"My Milanese ritual? Early on Saturday mornings, I buy cream meringues from Sissi."

Antonio Mancinelli, journalist and writer

FIND YOUR
MORNING ENERGY WITH...

A coffee and a Hungarian biscuit
Pasticceria Marchesi ●
via Santa Maria alla Porta,
11 – 20123 Milan
Tel. 02 862770
www.pasticceriamarchesi.it
marchesi@pasticceriamarchesi.it

A coffee and a brioche filled with cream
Pasticceria Cucchi ●
corso Genova, 1 – 20123 Milan
Tel. 02 89409793
www.pasticceriacucchi.it
pasticceriacucchi@hotmail.com

A coffee and a retro atmosphere
Pasticceria Biffi ●
corso Magenta, 87 – 20123 Milan
Tel. 02 48009702
www.pasticceriabiffi.it
info@biffipasticceria.it

A coffee and a pastry from Sissi
Pasticceria Sissi ●
piazza Risorgimento, 6 – 20129 Milan
Tel. 02 76014664

A coffee and a cream horn
Panarello ●
piazza San Nazaro in Brolo,
15 – 20122 Milan
Tel. 02 97378255
www.panarello.com
info@panarello.com

A coffee and a bit of gossip
Pasticceria Confetteria Cova ●
via Montenapoleone, 8 – 20121 Milan
Tel. 02 76005578
www.pasticceriacova.com
info@pasticceriacova.it

A coffee and a brownie
That's Bakery ●
via Vigevano, 41 – 20144 Milan
Tel. 02 8394890
www.thatsbakery.com

A coffee and a historic petit four
Pasticceria Sant'Ambroeus ●
corso Giacomo Matteotti,
7 – 20121 Milan
Tel. 02 76000540
www.santambroeusmilano.it

✓ **A coffee and an apple**
and cinnamon muffin
California Bakery ●
www.californiabakery.it

:-(cappuchino
luke warm,
cake stale

A coffee and an exhibition brochure
Giacomo Caffè ●
piazzetta Reale, 12 – 20122 Milan
Tel. 02 89096698
www.giacomocaffe.com

Discover new talent in a tree house

Some people grow up too fast and no longer have any interest in playing. Others put their imagination to rest after years of travels, because they feel they've seen enough. But others hold on to their childhood dreams, as they can create new worlds, even if it's somewhere that seems fine just the way it is. A place that adults can't reach, where stress doesn't exist, and which offers new and exciting vistas.

Chiara and Sylvie's story begins here: they brought together friends, new talent and their passion for fashion in a tree house. In the city. The project began almost as a game; friends all came together to display their handiwork. These little projects gradually transformed this weekend into a Milanese platform for up-and-coming creative talents. Here you can buy creations by new designers and vintage pieces and dance to a DJ set, wearing a small floral crown as though you were at a Nordic party. The location changes every year: check their website for details.

Chérie's Tree House ●
www.cheriestreehouse.com

Have lunch by a vegetable garden

Despite your best efforts, the geranium on your balcony seems to have wilted – oops! Not to mention the plant in the lounge, and the seeds you bought with spring in sight that have yet to see the light; you haven't got round to taking them out of their packet yet… Then there's the jasmine on your railing: it's time to call up the Protection for Plants Abandoned by Super Busy City Girls!

If you want to brush up on vegetable gardens and recover your lost green thumb, your destination awaits at the end of Alzaia Naviglio Pavese, just south of Milan. Alice, an American who believes in organic culture, decided to open up her restaurant in this quiet Milanese suburb. Here she has joined forces with a little community of local producers, who follow a way of life that works and respects the earth. Even in the city. The perfect place to sample dishes of seasonal vegetables that arrive straight from the orchard to your plate.

Erba Brusca ●
Alzaia Naviglio Pavese, 286 – 20142 Milan
Tel. 02 87380711
www.erbabrusca.it

DROOL OVER NEW BOOKS

Read in leafy surroundings
Libreria degli Atellani ●
via della Moscova, 28 – 20121 Milan
Tel. 02 36535959
www.atellani.it

Find a book on photography
from the
Armani Libri collection ●
via Alessandro Manzoni,
31 – 20121 Milan
Tel. 02 73318675
www.buchhandlung-walther-koenig.de

Good book selection, unwelcoming owners

Immerse yourself
in American literature
American Bookstore ✔
via Manfredo Camperio, 16 – 20123 Milan
Tel. 02 878920
www.americanbookstore.it

Leaf through second-hand books
with other collectors
Book market
in piazza Diaz ●
piazza Armando Diaz
www.piazzadiaz.com

Go for a classic
Books Import ●
via Achille Maiocchi, 11 – 20129 Milan
Tel. 02 29400478
www.booksimport.it

Support the oldest bookshop in Italy
Libreria Bocca ●
Galleria Vittorio Emanuele II 12 – 20121 Milan
Tel. 0286462321 / 02860806
www.libreriabocca.com

Relive the history of fashion
Fashion Library ●
via Alessandria, 8 – 20144 Milan
Tel. 02 83311200
www.bibliotecadellamoda.it

Binge on design
Triennale Bookstore ●
via Emilio Alemagna, 6 – 20121 Milan
Tel. 02 8901340
www.triennale.org/visita/bookstore

Step inside Charlie Brown's house
Milano Libri ●
via Giuseppe Verdi, 2 – 20121 Milan
Tel. 02 875871
www.facebook.com/milanolibri

Loose yourself
in new photographic images
MiCamera ●
via Medardo Rosso, 19 – 20159 Milan
Tel. 02 45481569
www.micamera.com

Flick through an eBook on a sofa in
an open space
Open Milano ●
viale Monte Nero, 6 – 20135 Milan
Tel. 02 83425610
www.openmilano.com

Spend your lunch break with your
favorite author in a lilac space
Il mio libro ●
via Sannio, 18 – 20137 Milan
Tel. 02 39843651
www.ilmiolibromi.it

Brush up on Italian literature

"Very, very offended, the world is very offended; whether it's more offended than us is hard to say."
Elio Vittorini

Your fingers are glued to your smartphone. You check Instagram compulsively and you always have your laptop on hand. But you devour books at the rate of a tweet, at night and during your lunch breaks. Or on the metro in the morning, as you try to hold your book up in a carriage that feels like a can of sardines, struggling to keep your balance amidst the comings and goings of the crowds of people around you.

If you're one of those people who won't hear of abandoning paper, you'll feel right at home here. Mondo Offeso bookshop is a haven just waiting to be explored, where you can rediscover Italian authors and breathe in the cultural air over a cup of tea.

Libreria del Mondo Offeso ●
via Cesare Cesariano, 7 – 20124 Milan
Tel. 02 36520797
www.libreriadelmondooffeso.it

Discover the world of
Les Copains in Milan

Les Copains ●
via della Spiga, 46
via Alessandro Manzoni, 21
– 20121 Milan
www.lescopains.com

Atelier Les Copains ●
via Alessandro Manzoni, 21
– 20121 Milan
By appointment only.
www.atelierlescopains.com
info@atelierlescopains.com

Become a child again

It's a Saturday afternoon in early summer. The days are getting longer, everyone's talking about the weather and how hot it is in the city. The usual chitchat. You're outside the entrance to the Padiglione d'Arte Contemporanea, perhaps after taking a walk in the Palestro gardens. Outside the museum there are couples, several families, and groups of people so taken up with their phones that these seem to be molded to their hands. The families set off towards a second entrance, which leads to a verdant area. You decide to follow them, but… stop! The sign is perfectly clear: ENTRANCE IS RESERVED FOR CHILDREN UNDER THE AGE OF 12 ACCOMPANIED BY AN ADULT.

Those lucky enough to gain entry will find themselves outside villa Belgiojoso Bonaparte, a large neoclassical building in the Indro Montanelli public gardens. The villa was commissioned by count Belgiojoso and became Napoleon's historic Italian residence. Today it houses the Museo dell'Ottocento. You can take a picnic here, and imagine the Milanese nobility wandering through the park, or Napoleon's relatives busy greeting guests who have arrived for an open-air reception. In such cases, a (small) chaperone is compulsory: talk about role reversal.

Villa Belgiojoso Bonaparte ●
Modern Art Gallery – Museo dell'Ottocento
via Palestro, 16 – 20121 Milan
Tel. 02 88445947
www.gam-milano.com

Take an excursion to a city farmstead

In the morning, you have your blueberry jam (only if it's organic, of course) on toast with your coffee – definitely one for Instagram. To be green in the kitchen, you opt for a pick of the local produce and make everything naturally and by hand. If you want to learn the map of the farmer's markets of the city by heart and discover that GAS delivers the best vegetables, this could be the place for you.

You will find yourself in a renovated farmstead right in the heart of Milan, a special place for a moment of peace and quiet. Spend your Sunday in a meadow, work on your PC outside or go food shopping in the evening. Or go for an aperitif at the bar and restaurant Un posto a Milano, where chef Nicola Cavallaro prepares his dishes using ingredients from small commercial farms and local producers. Go on a little excursion for an hour or so, without even leaving the city.

Cascina Cuccagna ●
via Cuccagna, 2-4 – 20135 Milan
Tel. 02 54118733
www.cascinacuccagna.org
info@cuccagna.org

Relax in a botanical garden

The second survival tip for Milan is to find your own personal oasis of peace. A place where you feel at home. Somewhere slightly hidden away, where you can cut yourself off from everything else and give yourself some me time. One such place is a historic botanical garden in the artistic center of the city, at the Palazzo di Brera complex, which is the headquarters of the Accademia delle Belle Arti. If you want to discover the place's origins, you'll have to go all the way back to 1774. Maria Teresa of Austria decided to transform the old Jesuit garden into an educational project surrounded by nature: an institution for medics and pharmaceutical students, where they could study medicinal plants out in the fields.

Wander among thousands of plants in this green open-air museum, such as the two ginkgo biloba imported from China in the 1700s or the peony and columbine gardens. The Braidense Library and the Astronomical Observatory are both within hailing distance: sit down with an ancient textbook or lose yourself in starry vistas. The gate is open from Monday to Friday, and entrance is free.

Brera Botanical Garden ●
via Brera, 28 or via Fiori Oscuri, 4 – 20124 Milan
Tel. 02 723201
www.brera.unimi.it/museo/orto
infobrera@unimi.it

"Milan wins you over with all the little details that gradually weave you into an eternal, poignant mosaic. But what I especially love is how multiethnic it is – it reminds me of New York at times, where I have stayed for long periods intermittently in the past.

Warsa, the Eritrean restaurant on via Melzo (at no. 16), is my favorite place at the moment. As soon as you enter it feels like night-time, because the windows are covered with African tapestries and furnishings. You could sleep there. You always need a bit of time to lose your inhibitions and start eating with your hands, but then the primordial instinct takes over and you really start to have fun.

They even have a vegetarian menu, they don't go easy on the spices, and everyone always smiles (with the whitest teeth imaginable). When I'm inside I enter a whole new world."

Debora Attanasio, journalist and writer

TRAVEL TO THE ORIENT

Destination Japan
Sumire ●
via Varese, 1 – 20121 Milan
Tel. 02 91471595
www.ristorantesumire.it
ristorantesumiremilano@gmail.com

Destination China
Mandarin 2 ●
via Benvenuto Garofalo,
22/a – 20133 Milan
Tel. 02 2664147
www.mandarin2.it
info@mandarin2.it

Destination Thailand
Bussarakham ●
via Valenza, 13 – 20144 Milan
Tel. 02 89432415
www.bussarakham.it
ristorantebussarakham@gmail.com

Destination India
Rangoli ●
via Solferino, 36 – 20121 Milan
Tel. 02 29005333
www.rangoli.it
info@rangoli.it

Destination Vietnam
Vietnam Mon Amour ●
via Alessandro Pestalozza,
7 – 20131 Milan
Tel. 02 70634614
www.vietnamonamour.com
www.vietnamonamour@gmail.com

Become little miss snob

A delicatessen on via Montenapoleone. The name might be misleading; if you're new to the city, you'll definitely be fooled. This place sounds like a shop from the fifties run by a specialist who busies himself advising women from behind an old-fashioned counter. However, it is now one of the most chic places in Milan: here you can enjoy exquisite cold cuts, accompanied by a glass of white wine in the heart of the fashion district. It's ok to bend the rules and treat yourself from time to time - right?

Once you enter, you will find yourself in the middle of a courtyard immersed in the history of the Bagatti Valsecchi museum. You can sit next to a fashion designer and their entourage or tourists who are just passing. Or perhaps elegant women who have just returned from an afternoon shop, like reincarnations of the goddess Kali with their Chanel handbags.

Il Salumaio di Montenapoleone ●
via Santo Spirito, 10 – 20121 Milan
Tel. 02 76001123
via Gesù, 5 – 20121 Milan
Tel. 02 784650
www.ilsalumaiodimontenapoleone.it
info@ilsalumaiodimontenapoleone.it

"My favorite spot in Milan is Quadronno bar, which never seems to change.
This place has such a friendly and welcoming atmosphere. I sometimes spend my evenings there, or I go for a quick Sunday lunch at midday. My favorite sandwich there is the Spalmatina. Today my only regret is that you're not allowed to smoke anymore!"

Valentina Crepax, journalist and writer

Give your opinion on an exhibition with a dictator

Don't be fooled by the name. This gallery, contrary to (linguistic) appearances, is a self-declared ode to freedom that houses unknown artists, big names from the art jet set and every form of expression. And maybe your own as well, whether you're a guest or just curious to learn what happens behind the doors of 47 via Nino Bixio.

If you're looking for somewhere that differs from the norm, you've come to right place: this gallery was born from the publishing project of Federico Pepe and Pierpaolo Ferrari. A young radical once came here to read her book under the covers of the bed in the window that directly overlooks the road. The gallery has played host to top male designers dressed as women, fashion bible directors who took part in a performance, and two radio presenters, who entertained an audience by wearing masks of politicians. On opening nights, socialites wander round pursued by the flash of cameras. Welcome to a new "Factory".

Le Dictateur ●
via Nino Bixio, 47 – 20129 Milan
Tel. 02 88007310
www.ledictateur.it

Radio Attiva
www.radioattiva.org
The city is their recording studio: every program is broadcast from a different location, well-known as *Jukebox On The Rocks* on the website of Rolling Stone Italia magazine. To keep up with the "radioactive" DJs on this Milanese traveling radio show, follow them on Facebook or search for RadioAttiva on Spreaker.com.

Watch a film under the stars

It seems like everyone's talking about this film; you've watched the trailer. During your lunch break, via a link on Facebook. That counts, right? As for that other film (worth a watch simply because it's got *that* actor in it) that won an award at Cannes – you've had a little flick through the making-of photo gallery. You really wanted to catch the third film, but as soon as you found a free evening, your nearest cinema stopped showing it. You can't wait to be able to spend a week in a room for your exclusive use with sweets and popcorn once summer starts. Then you can finally catch up on all the movies you missed during the winter.

Looking for a quick solution? Just follow the program for the summer screenings organized by Anteo spazioCinema, which transforms specially selected locations in the city into temporary open-air cinemas from June to September every year. You might find that it was worth the wait!

AriAnteo
www.spaziocinema.it

GET LOST IN A DESIGN LABYRINTH

Spazio Rossana Orlandi ●
via Matteo Bandello,
14-16, – 20123 Milan
Tel. 02 4674471
www.rossanaorlandi.com

Studio Museo Achille Castiglioni ●
piazza Castello, 27 – 20121 Milan
Tel. 02 8053606
www.achillecastiglioni.it
info@achillecastiglioni.it

Jannelli & Volpi ●
via Melzo, 7 – 20129 Milan
Tel. 02 205231
www.jannellievolpi.it
info@jannellievolpi.it

Arform ●
via Moscova, 22 – 20121 Milan
Tel. 02 6551448
www.arform.it
arform@tiscalinet.it

Danese ●
via Antonio Canova, 34 – 20145 Milan
Tel. 02 349611
www.danesemilano.com
info@danesemilano.com

Blitz Bovisa ●
via Enrico Cosenz, 44/4 – 20158 Milan
Tel. 02 3760990
www.blitzbovisa.com
info@blitzbovisa.com

Ventura Lambrate ●
(Don't miss this place during
Design Week)
via Giovanni Ventura, 5 – 20134 Milan
www.venturaprojects.com
milano@organisationdesign.com

"My favorite place in Milan is on via Crocefisso, in the courtyard of the Armando Diaz elementary schools.
A statue of Athena watches over the children here while they play. Standing between two ribbed columns, the goddess extends her arm, asking for silence to remember the fallen of the Great War.
The ensemble is agonizingly beautiful."

Giulio Iacchetti, industrial designer

Go to a concert in a restaurant boutique

Introductions can be so complicated sometimes. "What do you do" before "who are you", "where are you going" before "how are you". People reel off high-sounding titles and lists of impressive achievements, but by the time you get home, you've forgotten everyone's name. But there's no point trying to overcomplicate life. Indeed, the founders of this place only needed three words: travelling, products and food. Something simple. The space fuses these three concepts: it is a restaurant, a spot for acoustic concerts and a boutique, where dedicated young fashion designers come to sell their creations during the week.

You can have a quiet lunch in a room that looks out onto the inner garden, with the French-inspired kitchen in view. Or browse the shelves and listen to a young musician playing a guitar almost at a whisper, on a carpet set for a chamber concert. When the weather's nice, this is the perfect spot to enjoy an aperitif outside with live music. What better way to put you in a good mood than spending a blissful couple of hours here?

Gattò – Viaggi Robe Cucina ●
via Castel Morrone, 10 – 20129 Milan
Tel. 02 70006879
www.gattomilano.com

Join a secret society

You're in piazza Liberty, a stone's throw from corso Vittorio Emanuele. A focal point where voices and footsteps become one in the never-ending flurry of people, and where all the streets converge towards the Duomo. Suddenly, a door opens a little further down: the entrance to the Palazzo Spinola, at 20 via San Paolo. The sight that awaits you inside will come as a complete surprise.

This is a world within another world, like the wardrobe door of a Lewis novel. Here you will discover a hidden universe at a crossroads in the city centre, which has majestic halls lit with large crystal chandeliers. The largest room boasts three, arranged in a triangle like a triptych of light, with sofas, long tables and windows that open onto other rooms within the garden. From here you might suddenly catch a glimpse of fencers thrusting with foils – the perfect lesson of a bygone era. The rooms of this building are home to an ancient and secret society, which is devoted to fencing and fiercely protective of its exclusivity. Small tip: find yourself a fencing friend, and fast.

Società del Giardino ●
via San Paolo, 20 – 20121 Milan
Tel. 02 76020850
www.societadelgiardino.it

Drink from Hemingway's cup

"Excuse me, how do you connect to the wifi?"
"Why miss, you have another Martini!"

If you had to be won over by a digital access code, this would be the perfect way to woo you, with a twenties backdrop reminiscent of a Parisian café. Here you'll find the canal, jazz music, a young team and books waiting for you on the table, hidden inside the menu.

Which cocktail should you go for? Imagine you're spending an hour with Hemingway at the bar. He's drinking from a teacup filled with gin, spices and a little rose that is just peeping out from the top of his cup.

Mag Cafè ●
Ripa di Porta Ticinese, 43 – 20143 Milan
Tel. 02 45489640

"Two works of art in Milan create invaluable 'mental space' for me. Luckily they're on display in Milan, so I can go and see them as often as I like. The first one is at the Museo del Novecento at the Palazzo dell'Arengario, which has a spectacular room dedicated to Lucio Fontana up in the tower. It is home to the great neon work Arabesco Fluorescente, which was created in 1951 for Milan's IX Triennale. In one of his Manifestos on Spatialism, Fontana spoke about 'dominating the space, competing with infinity, putting a face to the invisible': this 130 meter high neon spiral sculpture interrupts and modifies the physical space. I often go alone, and I experience different emotions every time.

The Anselm Kiefer towers are at Hangar Bicocca, just a short stretch from the Arengario tower. This is a site-specific installation that was created by Kiefer in 2004. Here, like Fontana's work, the 'Seven Heavenly Palaces' create 'another space', a place for the mind that I really recommend you visit. You arrive from the impalpable neon fluorescence of Fontana to find several tons of reinforced concrete, lead, debris and sublime ruins, which forces us to stop and think. If you look carefully, you'll see that Kiefer also uses neon signs!

I'll let you discover other cross-references... everyone can have their own personal journey and transitional space."

Gloria Maria Cappelletti, curator and gallerist

FEEL REINVIGORATED WITH NEW VISTAS

Museo del Novecento
via Guglielmo Marconi, 1 – 20100 Milan
Tel. 02 43353522
www.museonovecento.org

PAC
via Palestro, 14 – 20121 Milan
Tel. 02 88465236
www.comune.milano.it

Hangar Bicocca
via Privata Chiese, 2 – 20126 Milan
Tel. 02 66111573
www.hangarbicocca.org

Artepassante – Theatre and Arts Atelier
Mezzanine on the Milan passante
ferroviario, at Repubblica metro stop.
www.artepassante.it

Massimo De Carlo Gallery
via Privata Giovanni Ventura,
5 – 20134 Milan
Tel. 02 70003987
www.massimodecarlo.it

Peep Hole
via Stilicone, 10 – 20154 Milan
Tel. 02 87067410
www.peep-hole.org

Assab One
via Privata Assab, 1 – 20132 Milan
Tel. 02 2828546
www.assab-one.org

Patricia Armocida
via Lattanzio, 77 – 20137 Milan
Tel. 02 36519304
www.galleriapatriciaarmocida.com

Lia Rumma
via Stilicone, 19 – 20154 Milan
Tel. 02 29000101
www.liarumma.it

Lisson Gallery
via Bernardino Zenale, 3 – 20123 Milan
Tel. 02 89050608
www.lissongallery.com

Museo Poldi Pezzoli
via Alessandro Manzoni,
12 – 20121 Milan
Tel. 02 794889
www.museopoldipezzoli.it

Museo Mangini Bonomi
via dell'Ambrosiana, 20 – 20123 Milan
www.museomanginibonomi.it

Invite yourself to a couple's home (museum)

This is a bourgeois apartment from the early thirties that was donated to Milan by a special couple: he was an engineer and she a ceramic artist, and they transformed their city residence into a veritable household art gallery. According to the museum wardens, after his wife passed away, the husband stopped collecting. He took it up again ten years later and pursued the passion that he and his wife had always shared. Paintings by Fontana, De Pisis, Morandi and de Chirico cover every inch of the walls of this spacious apartment. It is now run by a team of volunteers, who are supported by the museum operator of the City of Milan. You can visit this apartment-museum from Tuesday to Sunday, from 10:00 a.m. to 6:00 p.m.

You feel almost like an intruder in these intimate rooms, as if the owners might come back at any moment and surprise you in their home. This couple might be able to teach all art lovers a lesson: donating your house to your city is the greatest act of love.

Casa-Museo Boschi Di Stefano
via Giorgio Jan, 15 – 20129 Milan
Tel. 02 74281000
www.fondazioneboschidistefano.it

RITA WINES BY THE G

PINOT NERO IN BIANCO 12,5°   6
SAUVIGNON DOLOMITI 12,5°   6
VERDICCHIO SUPERIORE JESI 13,5°
VIOGNER MAREMMA 12°
SOAVE CLASSICO 13,6°
BIANCO DI CALABRIA IGT 14,5°
CHIANTI DOCG   13°
L'ACRIMA DI MORRO 13°
MONFERRATO ROSSO 14°
TEROLDEGO ROTALIANO 13,5
PROSECCO DI CONEGLIANO
CAVA BRUT 20 MESI

RITA TRUE ORIGIN

FILIPPO:
- BLOODY GAZPACHO

GAZPACHO, TEQUILA
& CONDI

CHIARA:
- FARGO

LIME, SCIROPPO DI ZAFF
PUNT E MES · SODA

FABIO:
- L'AGRESTE

MIELE, LIME, ACQUAVI
ROSMARINO

Savor a film by Bertolucci

You've just cycled along the Naviglio Grande at sunset; as usual, your bike heroically sees you over the cobblestones. You turn into a side street where cars rarely venture, and find yourself at the entrance to a secluded spot, far from the season's trends and fashions. Rather like those Bertoluccian travelers who hate being labeled tourists.

As you order your drink, you feel like Debra Winger in a red beret and round glasses, enjoying an exotic tea in the Sahara. Surprising new flavors and radical lifestyle changes await you, while a Sakamoto track plays in the background. Too far-fetched? Absolutely not: here you can savor classic scenes from Campari flavored Dolce Vita, a drink dedicated to Broadway star Mamie Taylor or the Olympic achievements of Lucien Gaudin.

Edoardo and his colleagues will be ready to greet you. The staff wander around dressed in green military uniform, as though in a film. The menu isn't a simple list; it's a small history book packed with references, film influences and quotations. The quotation on first page reads: *"Alcohol doesn't solve your problems, but neither does milk!"* Cheers!

Rita ●
via Angelo Fumagalli, 1 – 20143 Milan
Tel. 02 8372865
ritadrinks@tiscali.it

All hail tranquility

One of your girlfriends is really into yoga. Another is learning to master breathing techniques. Yet another has turned into the latest zen guru in the space of a few short months. How do they do it? You're one of those people who would be bombarded with bolts of lightning and words in nonsensical languages if you were given a speech bubble. The truth is that taking a break is always a huge luxury for Milanese women. You run in the mornings, even in your heels, or when you're carrying heavy shopping bags on and off the tram. You run down escalators. You arrive at the subway cars too late and out of breath; they're always faster than we are.

But two women have managed to draw breath in the middle of their hectic schedules, where running is usually imperative. This sanctuary is home to Katia and Paola, two old friends and career women who decided to change course after spending years on business trips abroad. Their place is on via Federico Ozanam, just round the corner from corso Buenos Aires. They took their experiences, travels and passions and transferred them to a little café, which they have since transformed into a lounge. Here you can drink a coffee or barley water and find that vintage dress that, coincidentally, was *just* what you needed for your wardrobe. In the summer, it's worth staying for the evening to listen to a vinyl DJ set or to hear a young writer presenting his first novel.

Pause ●
via Federico Ozanam, 7 – 20129 Milan
Tel. 02 39528151
www.pausemilano.com
info@pausemilano.com

Have a luxury breakfast

How can you reinvent yourself – in times of crisis – in a big city? First of all, pool your resources, like human file-sharing, so everyone can bring their interests and skills to the table. Then, set up a Twitter account and document the progress of your new project with photos and 140 character tweets. Get the camera rolling, pause for a moment, and then you're ready to go. This is the story of a copywriter, a pastry-chef and the founder of a start-up business. Luca, Giovanni and Diego decided to combine their common interests in a luxury haven at 27 via Felice Casati, not far from the Central Station.

Pavé is the place to soak up a simple yet very international atmosphere. An open space split into sections, typical of those urban sanctuaries where you can drink coffee sitting on the sofa, have a quiet lunch on your laptop or sit with friends at one of the long wooden tables. A word of advice: if you stop by for breakfast, go for the coffee and "brioche 160" combo. It's their specialty.

Pavé ●
via Felice Casati, 27 – 20124 Milan
Tel. 02 94392259
www.pavemilano.com
hello@pavemilano.com

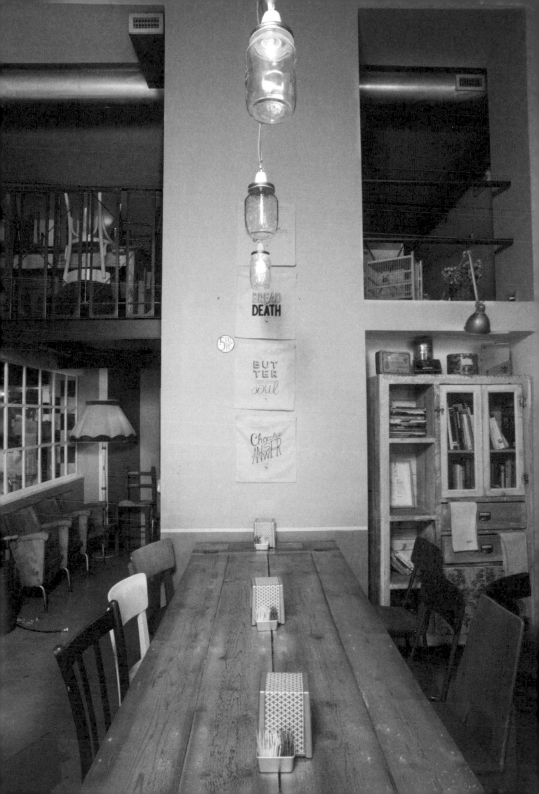

Feel as though you're at the seaside

The olfactory signal here is unmistakable. If you enter piazza XXIV maggio and head towards the Navigli, you'll know it immediately. And indeed, on the edge of the road, in front of the covered market and fruit and vegetable counters, you'll find a fish market that is *the* place to go for takeaway fish. This stand is open 24/7 and is the perfect destination for a quick, spartan snack. You can get fish fresh from the oven and eat it on your way to the subway stop at Porta Genova. In summer, it's a different story. Its small tables are packed throughout the day, and it's a great spot for a genuine, no-frills aperitif. You can have fried fish with a glass of white wine or an ice-cold beer, and enjoy the summer sunset.

For those who prefer something more classic, the Milanese cult offers the following: Luini's *panzerotti,* a stone's throw from the Duomo, Ginnasi's spit-roasted chicken, in piazza Bruno Buozzi, not far from Porta Romana. Then pass through the colorful cocktails and bamboo at the stands on piazza Mentana on your way to Gelateria della Musica. Be prepared to wait in line with your ticket, but trust us: this is the best gelato in all of Milan.

Il Kiosko ●
piazza XXIV maggio, 1 – 20136 Milan

Luini ●
via Santa Radegonda, 16 – 20121 Milan
Tel. 02 86461917

Giannasi ●
piazza Bruno Buozzi – 20135 Milan
Tel. 02 58321114

Chiosco Mentana ●
piazza Mentana, 20123 Milan
Tel. 339 523 1206

Gelateria della Musica ●
via Pestalozzi, 4 – 20143 Milan
Tel. 02 38235911

Go back to the good old days

A woman is sitting alone at a table in the corner. She leafs through that day's newspaper, which is held together by an old-fashioned baton. She has her bag and a soft drink next to her. Two regulars sit on wooden stools in front of the bar, chatting with the owners. No sudden noises, everything moves to the slow and calm wave of melancholy. If this sounds like your scene, you'll be welcomed immediately into a circle of like-minded people.

This bar bucks the trend of trying to be vintage at all costs; here, time stands still. And it works: everything is real, simple and no-frills. Like a good old Negroni, accompanied by one of the best toasties in Milan. They do things the old way here, even when it comes to the prices. Long live simplicity!

La Belle Aurore ●
via Privata Giuseppe Abamonti, 1 – 20129 Milan
Tel. 02 29406212

Treat yourself to a special break

Dine with a view of the Madonnina in the city's most fashionable department store
Maio Restaurant, La Rinascente ●
piazza del Duomo – 20121 Milan
Tel. 02 88521
www.larinascente.it

Relax on a leafy veranda
La Brisa Restaurant ●
via Brisa, 15 – 20125 Milan
Tel. 02 86450521
www.ristorantelabrisa.it

Play bowls at a Ligurian spot in Milan
U Barba ●
via Pier Candido Decembrio, 33
– 20137 Milan
Tel. 02 45487032
www.ubarba.it

Help a friend find a gluten-free menu
ISA e VANE – la cucina 2013 ●
via Perugino, 1 – 20135 Milan
Tel. 02 36515288

Dine with a celebrity
Giacomo Bistrot ●
via Pasquale Sottocorno, 6
– 20129 Milan
Tel. 02 7602 2653
www.giacomobistrot.com

Mingle with businessmen in the former headquarters of the Milanese carbonari
Boeucc ●
piazza Belgioioso, 2 – 20121 Milan
Tel. 02 76020224
www.boeucc.it

Have brunch in the courtyard of a terraced apartment block on the Naviglio
Turbigo ●
Alzaia Naviglio Grande, 8 – 20144 Milan
Tel. 02 89400407
www.turbigomilano.it

Go back to the 50s
Aromando Bistrot ●
via Pietro Moscati, 13 – 20154 Milan
Tel. 02 3674417

Feel at home with friends
Lile in cucina ●
via Francesco Guicciardini, 5
– 20129 Milan
02 49632629
www.lileincucina.it

STAY UP UNTIL THE WEE HOURS TO...

Listen to a DJ set
Atomic Bar ●
via Felice Casati, 24 – 20124 Milan

Drink the best
Bloody Mary in Milan
Cape Town Café ●
via Vigevano, 3 – 20144 Milan

Meet the new
queen of rap
Punks Wear Prada – Santa Tecla ●
via Santa Tecla, 3 – 20122 Milan

Discover your romantic side
Bar Cuore ●
via Gian Giacomo Mora, 3 – 20123 Milan
www.cuoremilano.it

Feel really boho
Jamaica Bar ●
via Brera, 32 – 20121 Milan
www.jamaicabar.it

Meet new people at night
during Fashion Week
Principe Bar – Principe di Savoia
Hotel ●
piazza della Repubblica, 17 – 20124 Milan
www.hotelprincipedisavoia.com

End your day with a Breakfast
Martini
DRY Cocktails & Pizza ●
via Solferino, 33 – 20121 Milan
Tel. 02 63793414
www.drymilano.it

Attend a (mini) concert
in a hostel
Ostello Bello ●
via Medici, 4 – 20123 Milan
www.ostellobello.com

Dance at an indie concert
Circolo Arci Magnolia ●
circonvallazione Idroscalo, 41 – 20090 Segrate
www.circolomagnolia.it

Get into an (indie) rock mood
Rocket ●
Alzaia Naviglio Grande, 98 – 20144 Milan
www.therocket.it

Have an aperitif to the notes of a vinyl
Vinile ●
via Alessandro Tadino, 17 – 20124 Milan
www.vinilemilano.com

Dance 'til dawn
Plastic ●
via Gargano, 15 – 20139 Milan

Relax in a thirties villa

It's early in the morning. A snow white villa and the green hues of the surrounding garden are bathed in a warm light. Suddenly the large front door opens: a woman descends the steps slowly towards the edge of the pool, like a silent, timeless snapshot. Meanwhile, beyond the gate, Milan is ready to begin its daily course.

You can soak up part of this atmosphere in one of the city's most beautiful oases of peace. This villa was commissioned by the Necchi Campiglio family and was built between 1932 and 1935 by Milanese architect Pietro Portaluppi. Today it is preserved by the cultural organization Fondo Ambiente Italiano. It is a real jewel in the heart of Milan and has a café next door. You can breathe in the refined charm of the old Milanese bourgeoisie, which has been a source of fascination for directors, photographers and curious passers-by. The villa continues to play host to productions, events and photo shoots for the biggest fashion magazines. When it's not inundated with the flash of cameras, it becomes a perfect retreat, where you can transcend time as you sip your coffee by the tennis court or the pool.

Villa Necchi Campiglio ●
via Wolfango Amedeo Mozart, 14 – 20122 Milan
Tel. 02 76340121
www.fondoambiente.it

Photo: Giorgio Majno 2008 © FAI- Fondo Ambiente Italiano

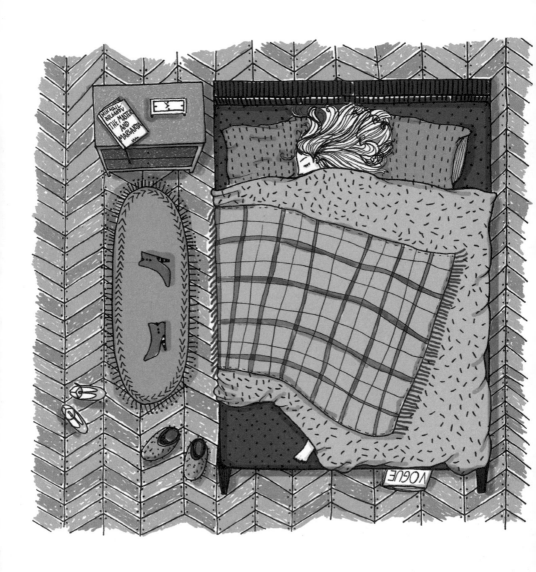

Buy made-to-measure furnishings for your room

Every day you promise yourself you'll change something. Upset the balance in your house, add another cushion. Or else remedy your urge to shop à la *Desperate Housewives*. Make an investment with a view to gaining the title of Survival Housewife at the very least. Never fear: there are three women who will come to your rescue. This trio has made furnishings and the search for the exotic their philosophy.

Your first stop is the historic Mimma Gini: a byword for Milanese tradition when it comes to textiles, which can be found at 11 via Gian Giacomo Mora. We then move on from here to the more exotic and naïve tones of Lisa Corti, queen of a color emporium at 2 via Lecco, close to Porta Venezia. Her story began in Africa: in Asmara, Eritrea, passing via Keren, before arriving in Milan and then on to India. The tapestries and Byzantine collections steer clear of the latest trends, and remain timeless and free of any dictates.

The tour ends with a special meeting at 4 corso Concordia. Here you will be welcomed by an elegant lady with a silver bob who will invite you into a real treasure trove of fabulous objects. Chantal Delorme, a native of Algeria and a tireless traveler, is now based in Milan and owns a shop filled with colorful glasses, jewelry, pottery and restored items such as antique furniture, French picture frames and art deco vases. Welcome to the court of the Milanese Furnishing Triad.

Mimma Gini
via Gian Giacomo Mora,
11 – 20123 Milan
Tel. 02 89400722
www.tessutimimmagini.com

Lisa Corti
via Lecco, 2 – 20124 Milan
Tel. 02 20241483
www.lisacorti.com

Chantal Delorme
corso Concordia,
4 – 20129 Milan
Tel. 02 799730
www.chantaldelorme.it

145

Meet a celebrity beautician

"What sets Milanese women apart from other women? They're always in a rush! And then their obsession with being on time: they always keep a close eye on the clock so they don't miss their next appointment. But they come here to unwind and indulge in a moment of total relaxation."

A native of Indochina, André Malbert has travelled to 47 countries to attend to the faces of the world's most beautiful women: Marlene Dietrich, Catherine Deneuve and Jeanne Moreau, to name just a few. He has given massages to top dancers such as Rudolf Nureyev. Today Roberto Bolle is a loyal client. During his travels in Monte Carlo, André worked behind the scenes with the Principality entourage for eleven years.

These days you can find this French beauty guru at Studio Estetico 11 on via Ruffini, with his French accent and reassuring voice. The beautician first launched his career in Paris, where he became Jean d'Estrées' protégé. From here he headed in the direction of Milan with *Biologique Recherche*, which chose him for its debut on the Italian market. He leads the life of a globetrotter, with beauty sessions, trialing of new machines and a technique that has made him famous the world over, thanks to the story that he tells through his hands.

Studio Estetico 11 ●
via Ruffini, 11 – 20123 Milan
Tel. 02 48513621
www.studioestetico11.it
studioestetico11@libero.it

Leave Milan for New York

Those streets that fill us with calm just by walking down them become our safe haven. Crossroads that harbor memories, electronic voices that accompany us on the subway back home in the evenings. But also those ancient stone women who support the entrance halls of the centre's historic buildings, and, in fact, the entire city. They seem to understand us; they observe and scrutinize our every move, day in, day out. It's much easier for us city dreamers to be unfaithful to a man than to our favorite part of the city - the area where we were born, the one that adopted us or that we're thinking of leaving (but we know deep down that we never will).

If you're thinking of being unfaithful to Milan, head to 46 Naviglio Grande. Your partner in crime for this adulterous act will be Tizzy, a blond New Yorker and one-woman show of a place that bears her name and the tastes of the city. Here you will find typical checkered floor tiles, free wifi and an all-male staff who speak in English and seem to have been specially cast for the role from a modeling agency. This is a favorite spot for foreigners in the city, the hub of a large international family, where you can eat a hamburger at any hour of the day and have a cup of American coffee whilst leafing through W Magazine. Ready for your fling with Mr. New York?

Tizzy's Bar & Grill ●
Alzaia Naviglio Grande, 46 – 20144 Milan
Tel. 02 58118227
www.tizzysbarandgrill.com
info@tizzys.it

CONTINUE YOUR MILANESE ADVENTURES ONLINE!
Follow My Secret Milan on:

Twitter: twitter.com/mysecretmilan
Instagram: instagram.com/mysecretmilan
Facebook: My Secret Milan Official Page
Pinterest: pinterest.com/mysecretmilan

KEY

Galleries

Museums

Nurseries & florists

Restaurants

Cinemas & theatres